**Genre** Fiction

 Essential Question
How do people get along?

Rainy Day

by Jerome Anderson
illustrated by Marcy Tippmann

Chapter 1 Rain

Jenna looked out the window and moaned.

"Ugh! It's still raining!" she said. "Now my day with Nikki is not going to be fun. I hate rain. It's so boring."

Jenna's cousin Nikki was coming over for the day. They had planned to play at the park. They had planned a picnic, too.

Rain drummed harder on the roof. "And it's noisy!" Jenna shouted.

Gran came into the living room. "Did I hear you describe the rain as boring and noisy?" she asked. "Sounds like somebody got up on the wrong side of the bed."

"I did not," Jenna said. "I got up the same way I always do."

4

"You know what I mean, grumpy-pants," Gran said. She looked amused. "The rain is good for the earth. You and Nikki can make other plans. Use your imagination."

STOP AND CHECK

How does Jenna feel about the rain?

Chapter 2 Still Grumpy

Just then, the doorbell rang. Aunt Susan and Nikki came in. They left their wet umbrellas by the door. Nikki was wearing rain boots.

"Look," Nikki said, holding up one foot. "I've been so patient. I've been waiting for months to wear these boots! The yellow ducks look just like bath toys. Let's go splash in the puddles!"

"I don't want to get wet," Jenna said. "The rain is awful. I want it to be sunny so we can go to the park. That would be fun."

8

"Maybe the sun will come out later," Aunt Susan said. "Until then, you can have a peaceful day inside. I'm sure you will find ways to stay entertained."

Nikki said good-bye to her
mother. Jenna sat on the couch
and pouted. Gran looked at
Jenna and said, "That's enough.
I know you're down in the
dumps about the park. But you
can still have a fun day."

Jenna sighed. She knew Gran was right. She was being kind of silly.

Nikki sat down next to her. "I like the rain," Nikki said. "But I'm sorry you're sad."

STOP AND CHECK

Why does Jenna pout? What does Nikki want to do?

11

Chapter 3 A New Plan

"Oh, it's okay," Jenna said. "Do you still want to go splash? I can get my rain boots."

"Sure," Nikki said. "And I have an idea for what to do then. We can have an inside picnic!"

"An inside picnic? How can we do that?" Jenna asked.

"We can get the picnic blanket and put it on the floor. Then we can make a picnic lunch. We can eat it inside. We won't get wet, and there won't be any bugs!" Nikki said.

"That sounds like fun," Jenna agreed. "We can splash around outside first. Then we'll make lunch. Can we make cookies, too, Gran?" she asked.

Gran said, "Yes! I love to see my girls cooperate. You go splash, and I'll get out the things we need."

"This rainy day is not so bad!" Jenna said.

STOP AND CHECK
What is the new plan?
How does Jenna feel now?

Respond to Reading

Summarize

Use details to help you summarize *Rainy Day.*

Character	Clue	Point of View

Text Evidence

1. How do you know *Rainy Day* is fiction? Genre

2. How does Jenna feel about the rain at first? Point of View

3. Use context clues to figure out the meaning of "down in the dumps" on page 10. Idioms

4. Write about how Jenna changes. Give details. Write About Reading

Compare Texts
Read about a group that helps kids learn and grow.

Boys & Girls Clubs

Everybody needs a place to play, learn, and grow. That's what kids do at Boys & Girls Clubs. The clubs are found all over the United States.

Boys & Girls Clubs give kids a safe place to have fun.

17

Working together is a big part of Boys & Girls Clubs.

The clubs are places to make new friends and to learn new things. Caring adults interact with kids of all ages.

Having fun outdoors is part of the clubs, too.

At the clubs, kids play sports and do art projects. They learn to be leaders and good citizens. The clubs help kids to be their best!

Make Connections

What do the clubs teach kids about getting along? Essential Question

How do both stories show people getting along? Text to Text

Focus on
Social Studies

Purpose To find out why it is important to get along

What to Do

Step I Find out about a group in your community that helps people get along.

Step 2 Draw a picture that shows the group. Share the picture. Tell what the group does.